What's Up With Me?

Puberty, Periods, Pimples, People, ~~Problems~~ and More

RED PANDA

First published by Red Panda, an imprint of Westland Publications Private Limited, in 2021

Published by Red Panda, an imprint of Westland Books, a division of Nasadiya Technologies Private Limited, in 2022

No. 269/2B, First Floor, 'Irai Arul', Vimalraj Street, Nethaji Nagar, Allappakkam Main Road, Maduravoyal, Chennai 600095

Westland, the Westland logo, Red Panda and the Red Panda logo are the trademarks of Nasadiya Technologies Private Limited, or its affiliates.

ISBN: 9789357761383

10 9 8 7 6 5 4 3 2

Book design by New Media Line Creations, New Delhi 110 062

Printed at Nutech Print Services Pvt. Ltd

TISCA CHOPRA

What's Up With Me?

Puberty, Periods, Pimples, People, ~~Problems~~ and More

Illustrated by Akanksha Agnihotri

Inputs by Dr Mala Arora and Malvika Varma

RED
PANDA

For Tara,
the light of my life.
I hope this book helps you and many other girls grow into strong young women.

Contents

Introduction

I desperately want you to know that you are amazing—exactly as you are—not a dot more, not a dot less!

Sometimes you may not feel like it, but trust me, I've been your age—you are an unbelievably brilliant and beautiful life with lots and pots of great things just waiting to happen to you.

But as you grow, you'll realise there is something common to all of us humans—it is change.

Perhaps by the time you are nine years old you've been told a million times already, 'You aren't a kid anymore.' And much as it may surprise you, it's true that things are changing—your body, the way you think, your behaviour, your equations with people, etc. Some changes happen suddenly, and some are more gradual. You may shoot up. You will gain weight or lose it and suddenly become lanky.

Hair will sprout in weird places, pimples may spring up on your face, and there will be other big and small changes. It could be overwhelming and even confusing. But the good news is it's not the end of the world, but a brand new beginning.

You are on your way to becoming a strong, powerful woman. And I hope to walk along with you as you take steps into this beautiful, new stage of your life. The idea behind this book is to help you with the right information and knowledge that will help make these changes smooth and even fun!

The book also talks about all the things that matter to you now—how to understand and deal with strong emotions, relationships with family, friends and boys. All this while making sure of your safety as well as the way to conduct yourself in life and online.

Actually, this book was inspired by my conversations with my eight-year-old daughter, Tara, and her friends. I realised it was time to break away from the old ways of referring to puberty, menstruation and the cycle of maturation all young girls go through, the world over.

Through eye-catching illustrations and an easy-to-relate style of prose, I want to reach out to all you pre-teen girls and your parents. I want to ease the often embarrassed, even non-existent conversations between your parents and you, who are on the cusp of one of the most confusing phases of your young lives.

I hope to give your parents a valuable tool too—a starter kit, that will allow them to learn for themselves and ask the right questions as they learn to navigate the beginning of your puberty. After all, being a parent is also new to them. I know it's sometimes hard for me too!

I hope you will know it's okay to be confused now. But as we discuss different aspects of growing up, understanding your body and the changes that you will undergo you'll get more clarity and the confidence to deal with everything.

Reading this book with your parents or friends will help you breeze through this time. After all, knowledge is power. Besides that, I also have a Tara, my daughter, who is almost your age, so I kind of know the questions you have and what you may be going through.

The information in this book is checked by our panel of experts—M&M (gynaecologist Dr Mala Arora and psychologist Malvika Varma). Dr Mala is one of the country's leading gynaecologists, and her daughter is a doctor too, in New Jersey. Malvika Varma is a kind and dear friend besides being a highly trained therapist. She has helped with some great suggestions about all the tough bits—moods, the strange new feelings pertaining to friends and family dynamics.

I look at you and hope with all my heart that you will grow up to be strong, courageous women who will bring joy and sunshine everywhere you go while making the world a much better place. Here's to your growing up with power, confidence and compassion!

CHAPTER 1

Get Set, Grow!

You've got a spark in you. You just gotta ignite the light and let it shine.

—Katy Perry

When my family and I first landed in Delhi, from Kabul, everything seemed unfamiliar and strange. This included my new school and classmates. I was in the sixth standard, and there were lots of hushed whispers about a lot of things—my strange accent and the P-word.

All my new friends had heard something about the P-word from their older cousins and friends. And here I was, just getting to know my cousins in India. So, it were my friends who first told me about puberty.

PUBER—what? It's *pew-burr-tee!* Okay, so the word is quite a mouthful. But I understood that puberty is the process of growing up that involves all those tiny little changes that would lead to me becoming an adult. I found out that both boys and girls go through puberty. But let's talk about what puberty means for girls, shall we? We can talk about boys in a later chapter ... because this book is for us girls.

What's Going On?

For girls, puberty normally starts between the ages of nine and thirteen, but sometimes it can be as late as fourteen or fifteen years.

Around this age, your super-smart brain sends signals to your super-cool body, and wham ... puberty arrives! The body releases chemical messengers called hormones that trigger a series of changes, some visible and some that happen very quietly inside your body. Your chest starts developing into breasts. Small, thick curly hair starts growing on parts of your body. And then there is the big event—the first period. Even though all these changes may seem bizarre now, rest assured, everything is going according to a grand, well-made plan.

Curious?

Go ahead and take a little peek at yourself in the loo. There's nothing to be embarrassed about! Look at yourself, with clothes or without, so that you are comfortable with your rapidly changing body. What is magical is that most of these changes happen gradually. Your body gives you time to get used to them. Puberty normally lasts two to three years, but it can be different for each of you.

Of Breasts and Bras

As your periods start (or sometimes even a little before that), your body begins growing in surprising ways. You may gain weight or height, suddenly. Your waist may become narrow and hips more rounded. Your breasts may seem bigger too. At first, it might feel awkward. You may feel self-conscious about your changing body and end up hunching to hide your newly developing breasts. Things that you earlier did without a thought, like jumping or running around may now seem super uncomfortable. But don't worry! You will eventually outgrow these feelings of discomfort and start loving your breasts. You aren't alone in this, these changes will happen to each and every one of you.

You may end up comparing your breasts with those of your friends. Some of them may have bigger breasts than yours and some smaller. That's completely normal. Some flowers are bigger, some smaller, some red and some purple. That's just the way nature is ... it loves variety.

Your kindness, ability to imagine and understand the world around you, and your amazing spirit will beautifully carry you through your entire life. And always remember that you are so much more than your body.

Once your breasts start growing, you will need to wear the right bra. Luckily, with different bras available for every stage of growth, you are spoilt for choice. There are training bras, sports bras, tween bras and more.

The Perfect Fit

Shopping for your first bra can be a great adventure. It's normal to feel a bit embarrassed or even a little excited. What is really important is to find the perfect fit. Too tight and it's super uncomfortable, too loose and it may not provide you with enough support. You should seek help from professional fitters, at lingerie stores, whose job is to help girls find bras that fit right.

Bras have two types of measurements. The cup size, or the size of the breast, goes from A to the very-rare M. And there is the band size, which is the measurement around your ribcage, under your breasts. A well-fitting bra cups your breast perfectly without overspilling or leaving room in the cup. And it isn't too loose or tight around the underbust area.

Wearing a lightly padded bra is a good idea because it stops your nipples from showing through clothes, particularly t-shirts. It's a great idea to go for bras that have a high percentage of cotton. Lacy bras look cute, but they can be uncomfortable.

It's a bad fit when:

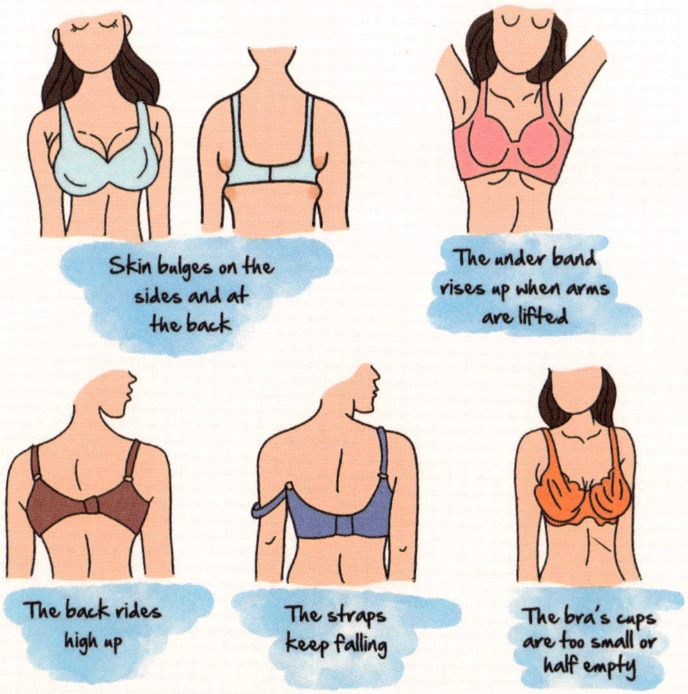

Hair and There

Puberty often brings along the attack of the hair monster. All of us have tiny body hair (called *lanugo*) all over our bodies which tends to grow faster and thicker during puberty. What may weird you out is the sudden spurt of hair growing on your arms, legs, upper lips, armpits and ... even on the area between your legs (called pubic hair).

The pubic hair is slightly thicker, darker and curlier. It acts as a protective layer and guards your private parts from injury and bacteria.

The time when pubic hair starts to appear differs from person to person. For some, it may be after breast development while for others it may be before. Different bodies, different timelines!

To Keep or Not to Keep

While body hair is entirely natural, if it bothers you, there are several ways to get rid of it. It is also perfectly fine not to.

I had a friend who was self-conscious of her 'moustache' and shaved it off with her dad's razor. Later, she had to deal with an angry red rash and prickly hair that grew back in the next two days.

Of course, this doesn't mean that you must live with upper lip or any other hair you don't want. But before making any decision, discuss it with your parents. The good news is that there are more ways to deal with body hair now than ever. From waxing and epilation to creams and lasers, you will have no problem finding a way that is just right for you. A beautician is the best person to suggest the best way to get rid of unwanted hair.

Sweaty and Stinky

When you suddenly start sweating buckets and notice a funny odour, perhaps puberty is just around the corner. With puberty, your sweat glands go into overdrive, so it becomes more important than ever to shower daily. Pay particular attention to the armpit and groin areas as they tend to sweat more.

One could use deodorant for the armpits after a shower. But please do not apply any chemicals to the pubic area because the skin down there is very sensitive and could react to the use of deodorants.

A very lazy classmate avoided showering and came to school after spraying a litre of her mum's perfume. But it didn't work at all because whoever sat next to her moved away real quick. You see, perfumes can't conceal body odour. Finally, a friend and I got her in a huddle and told the poor girl what the problem was. She got her shower game on, and the matter was history soon.

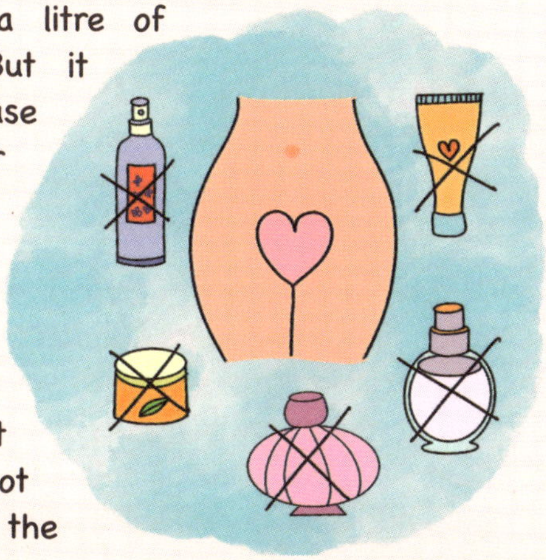

Trouble Spots

Pimples are the villains in teenagers' lives, or so they think. They look small but can become a big deal.

THERE ARE FOUR TYPES OF ACNE OR PIMPLES:

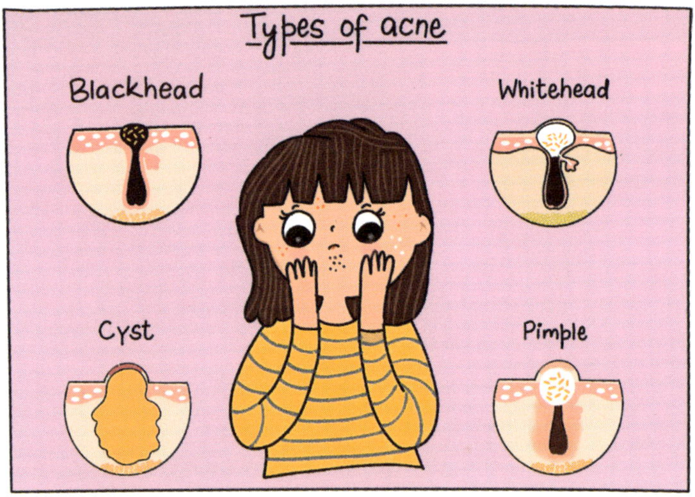

a) **Whiteheads:** Closed pores with tiny white bulges

b) **Blackheads:** Pores clogged with dirt; they are black in colour

c) **Pimples:** Red-coloured skin breakouts; often ooze liquid called pus

d) **Cysts:** Big pimples with deep roots; can lead to infections

Acne or pimples develop during puberty because the body starts secreting more oil, opening up pores on the skin. Dead cells, dandruff and dirt clog these pores and turn them into evil little pimples. If you are not careful, pimples can leave scars that can last a very long time.

If your acne or pimple problem persists, please consult a dermatologist.

Keep it Clean

- Gently wash your face with a face wash, twice a day.
- Don't over-wash or use harsh scrubs.
- Use products that won't clog your pores.
- No matter how tempting it is, don't touch your face and pimples. Your hands could be laden with bacteria.
- Don't ever pick or squeeze pimples. It can leave permanent scars.
- Don't sleep with makeup on as it clogs skin pores.
- Drink two to three litres of water to flush out toxins from the body.
- Avoid oily, sugary, starchy and junk foods.
- Wash your hair often to make sure it's dandruff-free.
- Cleanse your hair to remove residue of gels or hair sprays. Too many hair products can damage the hair and irritate the scalp.
- Avoid direct sunlight; it can aggravate pimples.
- Exercise regularly; toxins flow out via sweat.
- Stress causes pimples too—so chill!

Expert Advice

Growing Pains

During the pubertal growth spurt, some girls may complain of muscle pain in their thighs or calves. These growth pains are mild and disappear just the way they emerged. Some stretching exercises, vitamin D supplements, massage or a heating pad can decrease the pain. A doctor may be consulted only if the pain persists for several days.

Expert Advice

Dealing with Change

When you notice some of these changes happening to your body—like putting on weight, growing hair or developing pimples—you must remember that you are not merely the sum total of your body. You are a whole person, made up of many parts, and your appearance is just one aspect. Never judge yourself based on a single part. You are talented, intelligent, kind, friendly, funny, interesting ... no matter how you look.

CHAPTER 2

Body Basics

I think it's so important for girls to love themselves and treat their bodies respectfully.

–Ariana Grande

When you reach a certain age, your body starts preparing for an upgrade. And what an amazing upgrade it is!

The next stop? Your period!

But before we understand this really cool function, let's understand our body and the area 'down there' that we don't talk about much.

A Trip Down There

Around puberty, there is a lot of action going on in the area between your legs.

Growing up, I always assumed that girls have only two openings in their genital area. That there is a third one, came as a huge surprise. Well, this is what I learnt ...

Basically, girls have three openings in the area between their legs. The first, the anus, is for pooping. The second, the urethra, is for peeing. It is that part where you feel pressure when you are dying to pee.

The third and mysterious opening is called the vagina. The visible outer parts of the vaginal area are together called the vulva.

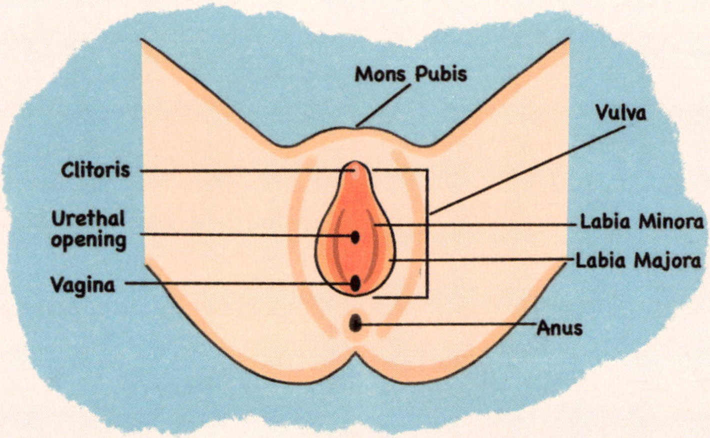

The vulva has a host of smaller parts. The lip-like petals that protect the vagina are called labia, the Latin word for lips. The bigger outer lips are called the labia majora and the smaller inner lips are called labia minora. These two sets of labia are protected by a fleshy part that ends at the bottom of your belly and is called the mons pubis or the pubic mound. At the meeting point of the two lips of the labia minora is a small button-like knob called the clitoris, which is super sensitive and feels somewhat pleasant to touch.

All these various parts of the pubic area are very interesting in design, each with a different feel or texture. The labia majora has hair on the outside; the labia minora has thinner skin and is soft; and the clitoris is small and fleshy.

A Journey Within

Now, let's go deeper inside, shall we?

The vagina is hardly visible until you go looking for it. Yet, it is a totally awesome body part.

Newborn babies come out from the vagina.

A newborn baby can be quite large; I'm sure you've seen one. One glance at your vagina will tell you that it's definitely way smaller than a baby. How do you suppose this works, then? Well, the vagina can expand up to three times its size to allow a baby to pop out. After the baby comes out, the vagina comes back to its normal size. Now, don't you think it's cool that you have a vagina?

Another fun fact is that the vagina needs no cleaning inside because it has self-cleaning powers! It produces fluids to flush out any bacteria, so there is no need to use products like soaps or body washes inside the vagina. In fact, doing so can end up creating a lot of problems!

Let's continue the journey inward. The vaginal passage extends all the way inside, to the cervix, which is approximately two inches below your belly button, inside the body. The cervix is the mouth of the womb. The womb, also called the uterus, is a pear-shaped organ in your lower abdomen, which is where babies grow when it is time. The womb then branches into two fallopian tubes that end in an ovary each. The ovaries are the egg basket of our body and contain little eggs, which are released each month into the uterus through the fallopian tubes.

These tiny eggs are the reason for our periods.

Let's talk about that in detail going forward.

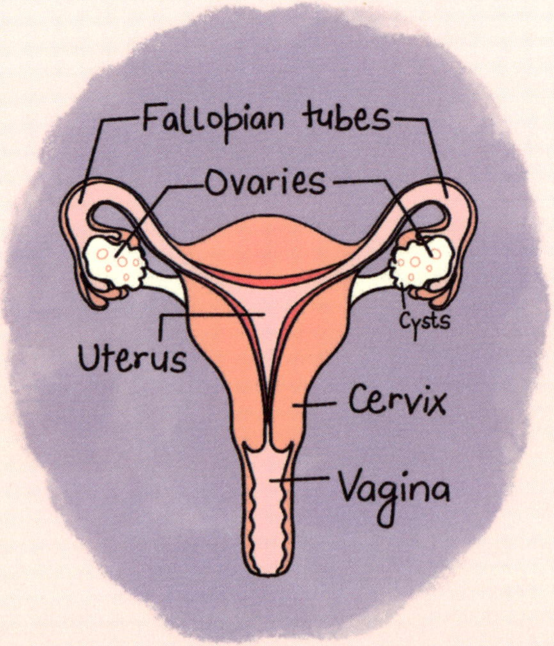

Expert Advice

Dr Mala Arora

The Science of Growing Up

A small master gland, called the pituitary, is responsible for producing growth hormones that trigger puberty. This pea-sized gland is situated at the base of the brain behind the bridge of the nose, and is controlled by the hypothalamus, which is a part of the brain.

At the time of puberty, the hypothalamus produces a hormone which activates the pituitary. The activated pituitary gland releases two essential growth hormones that cause the growth spurt—Follicle Stimulating Hormone (FSH) and Luteinizing Hormone (LH)—which result in physical changes and development of the reproductive organs in both girls and boys at puberty.

The FSH and LH hormones further stimulate the ovaries that start producing the female hormone estrogen responsible for the onset of periods in girls and progesterone that eventually helps them sustain a pregnancy.

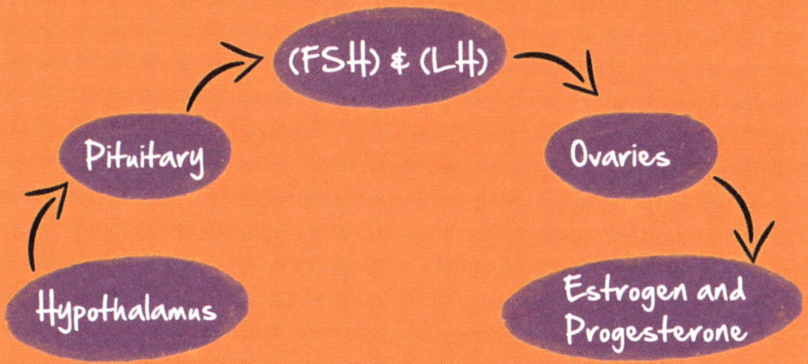

Myth Buster

It is far from the truth that sports can disturb the menstrual flow. In fact, exercise and physical activity can help relieve period pain.

CHAPTER 3

Go with the Flow

Don't try to squeeze into a glass slipper. Instead shatter the glass ceiling.

– Priyanka Chopra

Planning allows us to make the best of any situation. And undoubtedly, nature is the best planner of all. Look at how our periods are programmed in cycles of twenty-eight days, on an average.

So, what exactly is a period? Menstruation, the medical term for periods, is the flow of blood from your vagina. Getting your periods means that your body is capable of having a baby.

For us Indian girls, periods usually start around ten to twelve years of age. This is because of our hot weather. The timing of your first period depends on many factors like your family history, food habits and even the weather of the place where you live.

Seeing Red

I clearly remember my first period. I must have been around thirteen, and at school, when I noticed some spotting. Initially, I didn't pay attention to it. Back at home, I told my mom about it, and she hugged me tightly. Usually, a few spots of blood on your panty is the body's way of alerting you that your menstrual cycle is about to start. So, don't panic when you see blood, suddenly. Share it with your parents. They will be happy to know that their child is growing up healthy and well!

Sometimes, a few months before you start your period, you may even notice some white or pale yellow stains on your underwear. This is called a vaginal discharge, and is perfectly normal. It is produced by glands in the vagina and helps rinse out unwanted bacteria.

Other signs to watch out for are a feeling of heaviness in your lower belly, cramps and even a slight headache. You may also feel a little tenderness in your breasts or discover a pimple or two popping up.

The Drama Unfolds

So, what actually happens to your body during periods? Where does all that blood come from?

Your period is driven by your body's messengers—your hormones. So, if menstruation is the bus that's taking you through to adulthood, then a hormone called oestrogen is the driver. The release of oestrogen and another important hormone, called progesterone, triggers the start of your period.

Each ovary has millions of little eggs. At puberty, the hormones command the ovaries to release an egg every twenty seven-twenty eight days into the uterus. However, this could vary from girl to girl, depending on the body's rhythm. This phase, when the ovaries release an egg, is called ovulation. The ovaries usually release a single egg in one ovulation cycle.

Once released, the egg moves down the fallopian tube and drops into the womb or the uterus. Meanwhile, the uterus is busy preparing itself to receive the egg and develops a soft, lush lining called the endometrium. If the egg doesn't meet a male cell called the sperm and is not

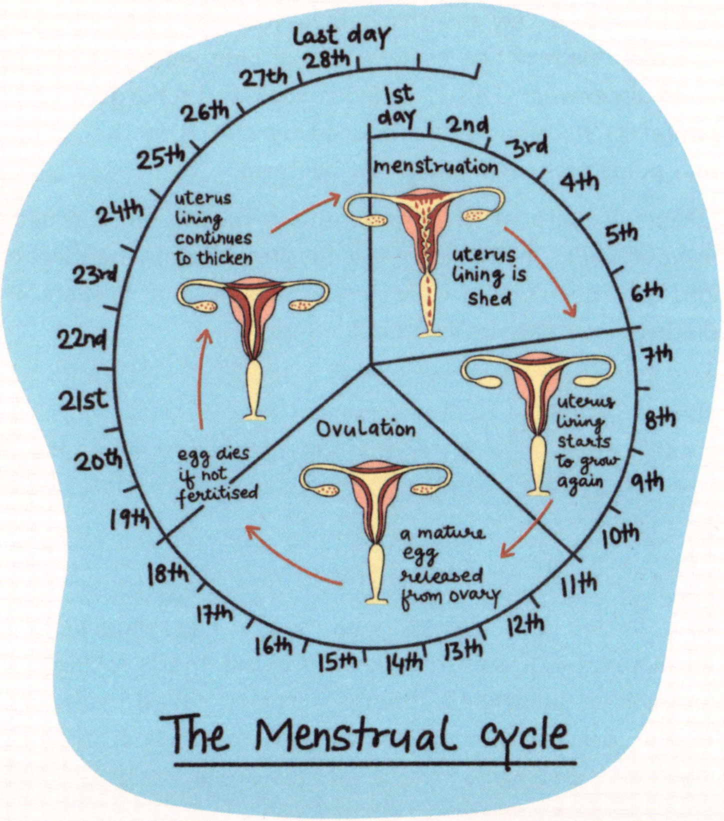

fertilised in the next ten to sixteen days, the soft lining breaks down and starts to flow out along with the egg. This flow is called your period.

The blood flow that comes out of your vagina is often brownish-red and may be a bit lumpy. Usually, the bleeding isn't much—maybe four to five tablespoons in three to five days. But you could have friends whose periods last up to seven days, and their flow may be heavier. For others, it may be over in three days flat. This is all good, though your levels of stress and physical activities may affect the flow.

What's the Secret?

Phew! So, there it is, the basics of your period, or menstruation. That wasn't complicated, was it? But then, why is it such a secret? Why do people act all weird at the mention of periods? They go around in circles, using terms like 'that time of the month', 'cycle', 'chums', 'leak week', and even 'Aunt Flo'.

This hush-hush behaviour has a lot to do with cultural taboos rooted in ignorance and a lack of understanding about what periods are. Sadly, not talking about periods creates more taboos, leading to a terrible cycle of misinformation. Which is why this book tells you everything there is to know about your periods so that you have all the answers first-hand. All certified by our two experts—Dr Mala and Malvika.

Myth Buster

It's shocking how many superstitions still exist around periods. In certain places, women are considered 'impure' during their period. The origin of this myth dates back to ancient times. Lord Indra slayed the demon Vritra, who was also a learned Brahman. After doing so, he felt extremely guilty. Indra then went to the womenfolk and requested them to take his guilt upon themselves. According to this myth, the monthly cycle of menstruation is a manifestation of this guilt. Of course, this is just a myth. With the scientific knowledge of why periods happen, we know there is absolutely nothing dirty, shameful or impure about menstruation.

Expert Advice

Essential Nutrients

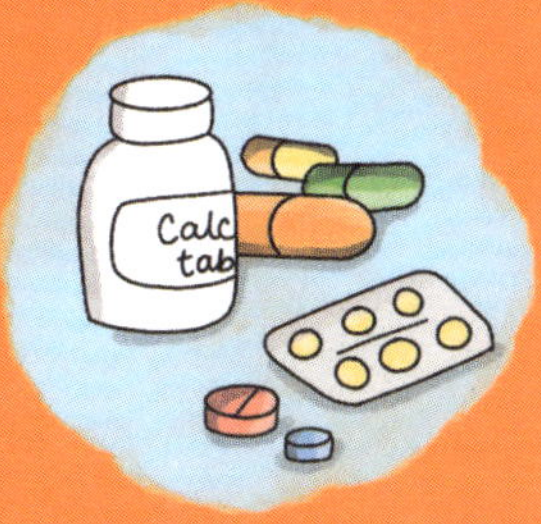

Calcium, vitamin D and magnesium are essential nutrients for growth and development during puberty. Calcium builds healthy bones and helps reduce fatigue, cravings and gloominess around this time. Vitamin D strengthens bones, muscles, teeth and the immune system. Magnesium helps manage sugar cravings and dizziness associated with Premenstrual Syndrome (PMS).

Expert Advice

Maintaining a Period Diary

Tracking periods ensures that you are never caught unaware without a pad or tampon. But more importantly, it helps keep a check on your menstrual cycle and issues like irregular periods. Using a period app on the phone is relatively simple, but it may require adult intervention to check how safe it is to share information. Using a diary is a safer option to note everything—the duration of your period, intensity of the flow, and other details like pain, headache or fatigue, mood swings, food cravings, and physical changes like acne.

Delayed periods are common initially, but there could be a hormonal problem if your periods continue to be irregular. For instance, high or low levels of thyroid hormone or being underweight or overweight can cause irregular periods. The doctor may conduct some tests to arrive at a diagnosis.

CHAPTER 4

The Period Toolkit

Sometimes it takes a thousand tries to win.

– Rihanna

I love wearing white clothes now, but I often dreaded wearing my white Physical Education (P.E.) uniform in school on Wednesdays. It brings back memories of some rather embarrassing moments. No matter how careful we girls were, someone or the other often managed to get a few red spots on their P.E. uniforms.

How, then, do you prepare yourself for this phase?

The trick is to have the right gear that will help you breeze through your periods. Thankfully, there are many options available, both in stores and online. Choose the one/s that feel most comfortable.

Sanitary Napkins

The line-up of sanitary napkins or pads available today is super impressive.

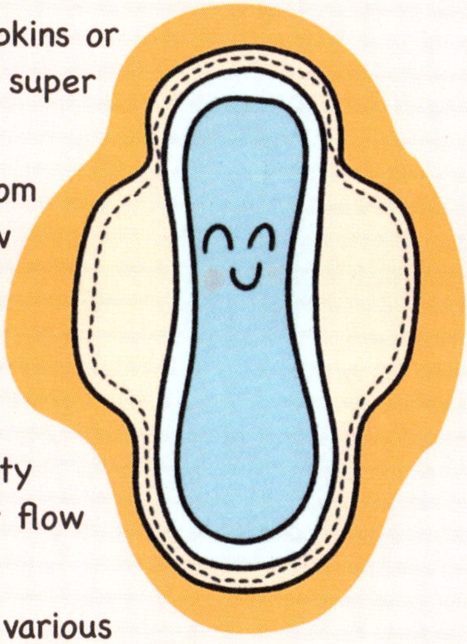

You can now choose from pads that suit your flow and feel comfortable. For days when you have heavy bleeding, there are 'maxi' pads. And then there are super thin pads or even panty liners for days when your flow is scanty.

There are pads available in various sizes and thickness for each one of you.

Other options include pure cotton pads and eco-friendly ones made out of corn starch and bamboo fibre. They are both comfortable and good for the environment, so do give them a thought when you are making a choice.

If you're ever in a pinch, you can even make your own pads at home. You just need to roll a few layers of cotton in a thin sheet of gauze, and you are good to go!

Tampons

Tampons are tightly packed cotton sticks that are inserted into the vagina and have a string outside for easy removal. They are super absorbent and soak up the blood, right at the source. They are a great option, especially when you are a very active person. If you're using a tampon, you might be concerned about whether it'll interfere with peeing. Relax—it won't. Remember, the tampon goes into the vagina, and you pee from the urethra (you can check back to the diagram on page 12). It is best to insert or remove tampons sitting down or squatting on the pot to have better access to your vagina and to adjust the position.

Period Panties

These panties can be worn without pads or tampons to soak up period blood. A fuss-free way to keep you

dry, they are a sort of girl-diapers that are less bulky. What's more, they can be washed and reused like regular panties. Period panties can also be worn with pads or tampons for added protection on days when your flow is extra heavy.

Menstrual Cups

A relatively new protection, these small, flexible silicone cups are inserted into the vagina to collect the period blood. Once the cup is full, you simply need to remove it, empty it and wash it properly before reusing it. It takes a little practice to get used to these cups, but they are more secure than pads, which means less stress about stains or leakage, especially while playing sports. They can be worn for up to twelve hours at a stretch.

Period Hacks

Back in school, we came up with our own ways to deal with stains that surfaced at the wrong time. We would rush to the washroom, wash the stain and pin the uniform skirt in a way that it looked like a design. Some girls intentionally spilt ink on the stains to camouflage them.

But here are some better ideas for you:

- It's best to carry either tampons or sanitary napkins with you at all times. The good news is that you can get very cutely-packed single units of both.
- In case you are not carrying one and happen to get your periods, most toilets have tampons and sanitary pads dispensers. So don't panic.
- In an absolute fix, you can create your own emergency sanitary pad by wrapping a roll of toilet paper around your hand seven to eight times.
- The flow at night is slightly heavier, so it's best to be prepared for overnight leaks by spreading a plastic sheet on your bed.
- Obviously, it is best to avoid wearing light colours during your period. Dark-coloured clothes and underwear are better at masking stains and covering up accidental leaks.
- If you are going to be out for long, you could be doubly sure by using a tampon and a sanitary napkin together.
- In case you are cramping very badly, it's best to get in some moderate exercise like a brisk walk or light yoga.

Menstrual Hygiene

Now that you are covered against stains let's chat about some hygiene around your periods.

- It is important to bathe every day and keep your vaginal area clean and dry, particularly during your periods. The chances of infection are more during periods. It is important to change your pad and tampon frequently because when you wear pads for long, even a little accumulated blood can attract bacteria. And do remember to wash your hands before and after every tampon or pad change.

- Since the vagina has an efficient way of cleaning itself, you don't need to clean your vagina from inside. But washing your vaginal area with mild soap and water is essential.
- During your periods, you may need to use the loo, including those at school and public places, more frequently. It is best to be safe and use a toilet disinfectant spray, wet wipes or disposable seat covers before using the potty seat. If none of these is available, it is best to line the seat with toilet paper.
- It's a good practice to wipe your genital area from front to back—starting from the vagina and moving towards the anus. Cleaning up in the other direction can lead to the spreading of the bacteria from the

anus into the vagina or the urethral opening. This could cause nasty infections.

- It's best to wear cotton panties during your periods since natural fibres allow the skin to breathe, preventing moisture from getting trapped. This guards you against rashes and infections.

- You can always use something like PeeBuddy, a stand-and-pee device, if you are travelling. That way, you don't need to squat or wipe seats. And what's more, it's disposable and eco-friendly.
- Never flush pads and panty liners in the toilet; you will clog it. The best way to dispose of used sanitary pads is to throw them in the trash can. If your packet of pads does not come with a small disposal bag, use some toilet paper to wrap dirty pads before trashing them.

Now that you know all of this, isn't it easy to work with your body and manage your periods? Your body is the smartest machine known to humans, actually. Even if you don't know exactly what is going on, your body sure does. So you can just plan a little and chill!

Did You Know?

In some parts of Ghana, West Africa, young girls sit under ceremonial umbrellas when they begin menstruating. The family gives her gifts and honours her like a queen.

Expert Advice

Myths about Tampons

Though there is enough anxiety surrounding tampons since they are placed inside the vagina, tampons are simple to use. Here are some tampon facts you can remember.

- Girls can wear tampons.
- Inserting a tampon doesn't affect any of your organs, including the hymen, a tissue found at the opening of the vagina.
- You can pee with a tampon inside as your urethra (from where you pee) and vagina are two different passages.
- A tampon can't disappear inside your body as the opening of the cervix (vagina's entry point) is too small to allow it to go elsewhere. You can wear a tampon and sleep.
- Tampons can't send the period blood back into your body when completely soaked. It does not cause endometriosis.
- The only thing to worry about tampons is that they can` cause toxic shock syndrome (TSS) if forgotten in the body for long. TSS is a rare infection that occurs when some bacteria get into the bloodstream and release toxins.
- It is important to change tampons every four to six hours.

CHAPTER 5

Menstrual Mysteries

Let life do its thing.
Be kind, work hard,
cheer people on,
and life will be
good to you.

–Camila Cabello

Winter or summer, having periods is the most natural thing on earth. In fact, not having it would be a cause for concern. If you find your periods are irregular or if you are bleeding excessively, then please ask your parents to schedule a visit to the gynaecologist.

There are several other things that you should know about your period.

UTI

Almost all girls and women will have a urinary tract infection (UTI) at some point in their lives, and summer months are when they are most likely to happen. As you know, the vagina and urethra are extremely sensitive and therefore infection-prone. The fact that we use so many different toilets in malls, theatres and restaurants only adds fuel to the fire.

If you have a fever and discomfort in the lower part of your tummy or an unusual discharge from the vagina, itching in your pubic area or a pulling sensation when you pee, do not ignore it. Please visit a doctor immediately.

Unusual Discharge

Vaginal discharge is quite common, both at the beginning and end of your period. The discharge varies at different times of the month—sometimes it can be watery and at other times, thick. This is perfectly normal since the vagina is doing a great job keeping itself clean and free of bacteria. However, if the colour of the discharge is dark yellow or green or it looks clumpy, please speak to your parents about it. It could be an infection.

Amenorrhoea

In all probability, you would have adjusted to the monthly rhythm of your period by the time you become a teenager. But if you have celebrated your fifteenth birthday and have not started your periods, it may be time to visit a gynaecologist. It could be a condition called amenorrhoea, which means 'no menstruation'. A few simple tests and the doctors will know exactly what's wrong.

Irregular Periods

Usually, periods regularise on their own. But sometimes they may not follow the usual twenty-eight-day cycle. If you don't get your periods every four to five weeks after you have had your last period, your cycle could be termed irregular. If you also happen to have very heavy periods (when you require more than one pad or tampon in an hour) or if a period lasts longer than a week, you will need to visit the doctor who understands your reproductive system best.

Cramps

Most of you will have some amount of cramping or a dull pain in your abdomen just before and during your period.

Contractions in the muscles of your uterus are responsible for these cramps. There is absolutely nothing wrong with that, and a hot water bag can easily take care of it. But if you are still uncomfortable, there are several safe over-the-counter medicines to make the pain go away. But if the pain still doesn't go away, it could be a sign of something a bit more serious like PCOD or endometriosis.

PMS

As you become a pro at the P-game, you'll realise that your moods will swing with your periods. As you grow older, you'll hear some people mockingly ask, 'Are you PMS-ing?'

You may feel sudden ups and downs of moods and energy as your body changes before your periods. Some of these may be quite drastic.

You may feel crampy and irritable or very lethargic. Your breasts may feel a bit sore and your abdomen and body may be slightly bloated. Cravings for chocolate or ice cream may also surface. These are all common signs of PMS. PMS usually starts two or three days before your period begins and should taper off by the first or second day of the period. Do indulge yourself a little bit; your body probably needs it.

If you can, try a few stretches or light exercises to help beat the symptoms.

PCOD

A few of you may have excessive weight gain or acute acne along with irregular periods. In that case, there are chances that you could have polycystic ovary disease (PCOD). It is a common condition which affects 10 per cent women in the age group of 12–45 years. Though the exact reason for PCOD is unknown, it usually happens when your ovaries develop follicles but do not regularly release eggs into the fallopian tube. Meeting a qualified gynaecologist and getting yourself diagnosed in such cases is very important.

In case you are diagnosed with PCOD, managing your weight, both with exercise and a sensible low-fat diet, will help control the symptoms. Avoiding junk food and regularising weight gain can correct the period irregularity and acne, even if you have PCOD.

Be a Period Pro

As overwhelming as it first seems, it is perfectly possible to become a total pro at handling your periods. Here are a few tips on how to become a period pro:

- Create a period kit with a couple of sanitary pads, tampons or panty liners, a small pack of wet wipes and a panty.
- If possible, keep a change of skirt or shorts at school.
- Exercising can help with period cramps. But keep it light for at least the first two days of your period. Yoga is also quite useful to fight cramps.
- A hot water bottle or a heating pad can help ease cramps.
- Having warm fluids like hot chocolate, a soup, or even hot water with honey will help deal with mood swings and keep the flow easy.
- Mood swings can also be managed with meditation and some deep-breathing exercises.
- You can also schedule activities you enjoy, like meeting your friends and watching a movie to keep yourself distracted.
- Your period may bring with it a mild body odour, so make sure to shower frequently and carry a deodorant.
- Eat light and eat right, since your intestines work less efficiently during this time.
- You may feel drained of energy, so it's best to get a little more rest.

Expert Advice

Endometriosis

While most girls feel discomfort and some pain during their periods, some may experience severe cramps around this time. It could be due to a condition called endometriosis. This results from some period blood leaking backwards into the tummy.

The most common symptoms of endometriosis are painful periods, pelvic pain or lower back pain.

Keeping a pain diary helps determine whether the pain during your periods is increasing every month. Please note the intensity of pain from one to ten, the location and duration of pain, how many months you have been experiencing it, and what helps relieve it. This will help your gynaecologist in their diagnosis.

Menorrhagia

It is fairly normal to have a heavy flow during some days of your period. However, if you have extremely heavy flow or prolonged duration of bleeding, it is termed menorrhagia. If a period lasts longer than seven days, or you have to change your sanitary napkin every one or two hours, it may be wise to consult a doctor. While hormonal imbalance is the most common cause of menorrhagia around puberty, other medical conditions may need to be excluded by the doctor.

Did You Know?

In some south Indian communities, girls' first period is celebrated as **'Ritusuddhi'**. Girls dress up in the traditional half-sari and receive gifts and gold as presents from their families. Women from the extended family and neighbourhood are also invited for the feast.

CHAPTER 6

Will I Be Pretty?

Be brave and fearless to know that even if you do make a wrong decision, you're making it for good reason.
—Adele

Beauty is something you and your friends will chat about a lot when you are growing up. Often, the subject of conversations is how much better-looking someone else is.

Sometimes one just doesn't feel good-looking enough. You may find yourself obsessing with one or another body part, thinking it is far from perfect. That is absolutely alright! I used to be so self-conscious about my body that I didn't focus on the good things about me—like my eyes or my smile. I kept thinking I wasn't normal.

That brings me to the question of normal—what is normal? Why is that normal and who said it is normal? I have been scanning bookshops for years but am yet to find the 'Normal Rulebook'. So, what is 'normal' keeps changing and to fixate on it is really foolish.

I have had the privilege to work with some of the most 'good-looking' people in the country, and I can assure you that they are a product of a lot of hard work. They not only keep fit with a lot of exercise and eating right, but there's also an army of makeup artists, hairdressers and stylists that helps them look the way they do.

The one thing that makes people truly beautiful though is that they are confident about themselves. They are aware of their weaknesses too, but they choose to highlight their best parts with a lot of joy. Happy people are beautiful people. Confidence actually makes people look beautiful. Think about it, have you ever seen an ugly, smiling face?

Just fixating on one body part can lead to total misery.

Discover Your Uniqueness

Ultimately, what makes you beautiful is what is unique to you. For example, a crooked smile or a dimple on your chin; anything that makes you, YOU.

Physical appearance is one thing, but the way we behave often makes people want to know us better. You may find that people are attracted by a crazy sense of humour, clever one-liners or sometimes just being the kindest and most compassionate person in the room.

So, my suggestion to all of you, who are struggling with your bodies that are growing into adulthood at this point, is to think about yourselves as being more than just a body. Rather, be a spirit inside a body. The body can keep shaping up in many ways as you evolve into an adult. But the more important thing is to look inside and see if you have the stamina—both physical and emotional. Do you have patience, kindness and tolerance? Have you acquired any knowledge of our world and its people? Are you brave enough to try new things? Are you courageous enough to stand up for things that you believe in? Those are the things that will stay with you even when you are seventy-five years old and have tons of silver hair and probably have passed this book on to your granddaughters. So, I would suggest, please don't get stuck too much with what is pretty, what is normal and trying to fit in. Discover yourself.

Fa(c)t of the Matter

The world is obsessed with fat and thin. Trust me, I've been there. I was a chubby pre-teen. I used to ask my father if I was too fat because somebody in school had called me *moti*. My poor father didn't really know what to say because it was pretty evident that I was overweight. He said there wasn't anything that I couldn't do anything about. He suggested that I start walking with him for an hour every day.

So, I started walking a lot. I lost a lot of weight, and that made me very happy. But what thrilled me, even more, was that I had achieved it with hard work and focus.

You can be a far fitter version of yourself. And thinking fit or unfit rather than fat or thin is smarter.

Let's get this straight, there is no perfect. There is no ideal body shape. Your perfect body shape is the one you have right now. It's the way nature intended you to be. Do not allow anyone to body shame you by calling you *moti*, *sukdi*, *lambu* and *shortie*. Tell them loud and clear that you are perfect, exactly as you are.

Food for Thought

In a previous chapter, we talked about not getting into the habit of overeating junk or fried food. Those certainly can't be good for anyone at any age.

Most food is just food—what makes it good or bad is how much and when you are eating. Of course, if you are eating a pizza on that one day you've planned to have fun with your friends, there's no point in thinking about how fat you are going to become.

One meal of pizza occasionally is not going to make anyone fat. It's only when you regularly consume junk food that it starts to become an addiction.

That is something you need to watch out. Sugar and fat are both huge addictions, and studies tell us that these start early in our life. So, if you are getting to the point where you can't manage without something sweet or fried, you should ask your parents to take you to a nutritionist.

Eating healthy is the best investment you can make at your age.

Here's a list of some cool fun foods that are healthy and fun to make with parents:

- Cottage cheese (paneer) burger
- Vegetable pasta
- Chicken or vegetable roti wraps
- Pita bread pockets with beans, olives and salad leaves
- Whole wheat sandwiches

- Whole wheat pizza with vegetables (and less cheese)
- Omelette loaded with vegetables

Keep aside a day a week to enjoy your fries, burgers and pizzas. But on other days, make sure to eat your vegetables, fruit, nuts and seeds. Carbohydrates, proteins and minerals are essential for you to have a healthy and fit body.

Hey, 'Pretty' Woman

Beauty is a huge business—it's a multibillion-dollar industry.

We live in times where almost everyone wants to take pictures of every single living moment and see how everyone react to them. You may be surprised by adults obsessed over likes, shares, subscribers and followers.

I find everyone trying to look very similar, but that is a little scary. Nature intends for us to be like a bouquet where every flower brings a different texture, shape and fragrance; when put together, that mixed bunch of flowers is the most beautiful thing you can see.

However, each of us has gone through a phase where we want to look like our favourite pop or film-star.

A dear niece of mine is obsessed with Katy Perry, and she keeps trying to imitate her in every way possible. I tell her she isn't blonde or American and it looks really weird. But then, I forget, I had my own Madonna-phase. And she

is just as American.

Besides, then there are a whole bunch of social media influencers who look so glamorous! And they aren't even filmstars, just girls like you, right?

What we forget is that the pictures they put out on social media are one among fifty other that they would have shot. I know that because I am on Instagram! I take so many pictures but choose the one I think is best and put it up, assuming that everyone will think this is how I look when I wake up. That's not the truth. It is far from it.

Don't become under-confident about things or areas of yourself that you think aren't perfect.

I suppose it is okay to wear kajal or a little lip balm if you are going to a family wedding or are in a school play. But applying excessive makeup when you are young can ultimately end up destroying your skin. And you need to avoid using chemicals on your face for as long as possible.

One of my biggest beauty secrets, and one that I share with anyone who will listen, is to never sleep with anything on your face, not even kajal. I wash my face squeaky clean and just apply moisturiser before I sleep.

If you are happy, everything looks gorgeous. Even your flaws start to shine and look like unique little qualities.

However, even if you've read all of this, you may still feel a bit awkward about yourself because it is a natural part of growing up. Nothing can take away that anxiety; it comes with your age. You must know that when you look back at your pictures when you are older, you will wonder why you didn't love yourself even more. You are full of love, life, intelligence, energy, charm and fun at this age. So please remember that you will always be the most gorgeous person to those who care about you.

Expert Advice

Dangers of Conditional Self-worth

Worth is the value given to something; self-worth is the value we give to ourselves. Conditional self-worth is when we attach certain conditions to our worth and value ourselves only if we fulfil these conditions.

Consistently meeting tough conditions—'I must be good at sports', 'I must get good grades', 'I must have the perfect body'—is humanly impossible. If we only allow ourselves to feel good when we meet certain conditions, we give ourselves conditional self-worth. So, when we fail to meet these conditions, we put ourselves down and think of ourselves as worthless.

A better idea is to aspire for unconditional self-worth. Rate your behaviour or performances in different aspects of your life and work on improving them if you want to, but NEVER rate yourself as good or bad. What gives us worth is the fact that we exist.

We should always remember that as humans, we are fallible, complex, unrateable and changeable. Never put yourself down for things that make you human.

CHAPTER 7

The Family Saga

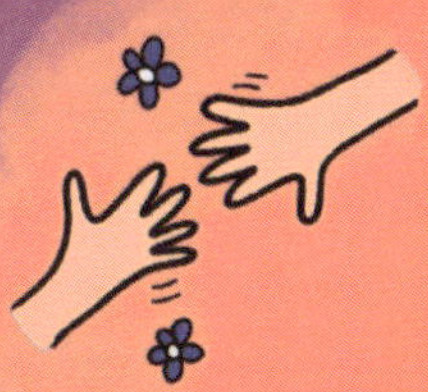

You can't let the highs make you feel overconfident, nor can you let the lows be a reason to dampen your spirits.

-Saina Nehwal

They say you can choose your friends but not your family. Sometimes it seems like you just can't get far enough from your mom, dad or elder sibling.

Then why do we treasure families?

The reason families are so important is because they keep us safe in this big bad world. Your family, weird as they might seem to you, will still be there for you if anything were to happen to you.

You are here because of your parents and grandparents. And on that note, let's talk a little bit more about families.

Hands That Rock the Cradle

Growing up, it seems like parents are your enemies. Let's get this straight—they aren't. Even if you may *strongly* feel so at times.

As you develop a mind of your own, your parents have a hard time understanding that you are growing up too. To them, you are still their little baby. The best thing to do is to have a *long* chat with your parents and *explain* what is on your mind.

Many families I know have meals together, particularly dinner, and find out what's going on with each member.

Some families do weekend outings. The time that you spend together is the time you need to discuss what is bothering you. Explain your point of view and request that they try to understand it.

Once you have made your point, give your parents time to digest what you have said and to act on it. If you can't get them around to your way of thinking, have another conversation and explain it another way. Maybe you can get them to chat with a friend's parent who has been permitted to do what you seek. Or promise to keep your end of the bargain and then get them to agree.

The one thing you cannot ever doubt is that your parents love you and want the best for you. There is no rulebook for being a better parent, so they are also figuring it out with you.

Their biggest concern is to make sure you are safe at all times. Your parents see you as an extension of their own life. You will understand this when you have kids of your own.

Papa Don't Preach

Constant lectures about what, who, when, where, why and dos and don'ts of all kinds can get annoying. But, for once, if you were to follow your parents' advice and see what happens, you may find that most of it is just good common sense.

Things like cleaning your room, finishing your homework on time and taking care of your personal hygiene are good habits that will help you when you are older.

Good habits formed at your age are essential for leading a simple life, instead of struggling to break your bad habits later. While you are growing up, you can change easily.

Discipline isn't the easiest thing to understand when you are young because it feels like a restriction. It feels like you aren't *free*. Actually, discipline is the best form of freedom.

Once you have good habits, you no longer have to force yourself to do things that are good for you. They become second nature.

Your parents want you to have the best life, so they try and encourage you to have the best habits that they perhaps struggled with themselves.

Kin or Kin-dread

Having siblings can be a blessing from heaven if you get along, or a curse from hell if you don't. In all probability, your feelings for your siblings will change many times as you are growing up.

If you are older, you'll find your younger sibling super annoying. They tag along *everywhere* and copy *everything* you do. If you are younger, you may wonder why your sibling is constantly trying to get rid of you and why they won't share their things with you.

At ten, any age gap seems huge, but when you are twenty-year-olds, someone two to three years older or younger will and can become your best buddy. You have so much in common—your parents, house, pets, maybe your school and, of course, your genes. That is such a great place to begin a friendship forever!

People close to their siblings can perhaps get along with many people and could be less selfish because they have had to share everything since they were little.

Sometimes you and your siblings could be competing for your parents' attention and affection. This is so normal. But parents can't pick favourites because for them their children are like stars in the sky ... each one is precious and unique.

It's best to chat with your siblings and make some ground rules about sharing. It's best to respect each other's way of thinking, even if it's not the same as our own.

Your years together are so precious! When you grow up, you may have families of your own. You may live in different cities or even continents and will not always be able to meet when you like. Your childhood *masti* will be one of the most precious times of your life. Trust me on this!

Fight Club

Our neighbours are a loud and feisty family. They fight in three languages because their kids are educated in America, the mother and father speak English and Hindi, but the grandparents only speak Punjabi. What we overhear is loud, funny and mixed up. When we meet them outside their home, you can't imagine a more loving family. Most families are a little like that. We rub each other the wrong way, get in each other's faces and feel no need to be polite to each other. We say what we feel like, when we feel like it. Isn't that great? To be in one's emotional night suit, comfortable and familiar with this small group of people.

Fights or arguments in the family don't last because there is trust. Remember that word—*trust*. It is the backbone of a family unit.

You know beyond everything else that you can trust your family. Your family will keep your secrets and have your back, always. Of course, it goes without saying that you will be trustworthy too, and won't just expect it from your family members.

The benefits of strong family bonds are one of the reasons Indians, Chinese and Italians do so well in the world.

Imagine having therapists, super cooks, best friends, fashion designers and financial advisors all rolled into one unit that is at your disposal. I can't imagine a better support system! Can you?

Saying Sorry

Ego often becomes the biggest problem in families. It is that part of you that feels a rise or fall in self-importance. If your parents scold you in front of your friends, your ego feels bad. The same scolding wouldn't feel so bad if you guys were alone at home, right?

The same is true of parents. If you disobey or are rude to your parents in front of their friends, they will also have the same feeling.

Saying sorry is not just something you have to do; parents could also apologise if they have hurt you.

Let's get this straight, you love your parents, and they love you more than anything in the world. So, in a long lifetime, if we hurt our family sometimes, I guess that's okay. But to let that become a big deal and not say sorry is just very silly.

A good rule that I follow is never to sleep on a fight. Never go to bed without making up. It's best for everyone!

Expert Advice

The Not-So-Perfect Family

Have you ever wished for a perfect family? I know I have! A family where everyone stays in harmony, there are no arguments or fights, all speak to each other with love, and everyone is always happy. Sounds divine, right? Or does it? When there are problems at home, we tend to wish for the perfect family, without realising that no family is perfect and cannot be. 'Perfect' means something is as good as it can possibly be, which means that there is no way for something to be better. Do you think this is true for anything? No, right?

All of us are imperfect, and that is perfect! Families come in all shapes and sizes—some live together, some live apart—and are made up of imperfect people going through various imperfect situations together. Think of your favourite TV shows, movies or cartoons. Do the families there seem perfect? Probably not. Yet you love watching them together!

Families have their strengths and weaknesses—some things that are good about them and some things they can improve on. They make mistakes and also make amends. Sometimes we let our emotions rule our actions and at other times, we think and act. There are good days and bad days for all of us in a family. And all these things make your family, interesting and unique. Focus on how you can add goodness to your family, and it will come back to you.

CHAPTER 8

Best Friends Forever

Friends are like diamonds. Fake ones look okay but they're cheap. The real ones last forever.

-Lady Gaga

At your age, friends are more precious than food, dresses, games and even parents!

We've all been through that stage where snacking, dressing up, sleepovers and all the other mad stuff is more exciting with friends.

Then suddenly, it's not. The same friend who you imagined being your best friend for life, starts acting weird. You can't stand them. And they, you!

It may seem hard, but remember you and your friends may be developing at a different pace. Your feelings are mixed up at this time—you may feel moody and upset at things you would have laughed at earlier.

It's a time for change, and we all know that change can be difficult.

Matched Mates

To have a bestie is great, but sometimes the *right* person isn't keen on being your friend. Maybe she already has her group figured out.

It may also happen that suddenly the best friend

you've had for years, talks only about boys. And all you want to do is watch a movie or play a game. Having one person meet all your friendship needs is really difficult.

They have their own thing, and so do you. It's sensible to have a few good friends so you can enjoy different things with different people. It doesn't mean you aren't besties. It actually means that you are such good friends that no matter who else you meet, you'll continue to love each other dearly, like the best of friends.

Frenemies, Seriously?

Some people *seem* to be awesome one day, and so weird another day. You get a feeling that they aren't really your friends.

They could be nice to your face but talk crap behind your back. They could be competing with you. There is a word for such people—frenemies. You probably already have such a friend, it's perhaps the one you are confused about. It's also the one your mother doesn't like too much. Yes, most times, mothers have a good idea of what's going on.

Friends can mean comfort and kindness. They are supposed to make you feel safe and be loyal. Friends, if they are the wrong kind, can also mean heartbreak and pain.

The best thing you can do is to let such a person be and minimise contact. It is much better to be alone than with someone who causes you pain. After all, being one's own best friend is great; you'll always have company.

Also, make some time to think about how you are as a friend. Are you being selfish, always wanting things your way? Remember, you'll only attract the kind of people you are. So, it's best to try and be a better friend yourself too.

Fight or Flight

Have you noticed how most fairy tales have princesses that need a prince to rescue them? You may no longer watch princess-y stories, but the idea may have been planted in your head that you need rescuing. Uproot it right away.

In my experience, most girls I meet do not need being rescued. They are warriors who are capable of defending not just themselves but anyone else who needs it.

Bullying is So Bleh

Sadly, most of you have either been bullied, have seen someone being bullied or have bullied someone. While it is all a part of growing up, what's really cool is, stopping a bullying episode, since it can have terrible effects that can last for many years, even after the bullying has stopped.

Pushing, shoving and saying nasty things are some mean things bullies do. And when you feel someone is using their power to hurt you, again and again, it's time to call out their game. Never ever let a bully make you believe you are lesser than them. Stand up for yourself and your friends if they are being bullied.

Saying, 'Stop it. I won't be bullied,' could get a bully to back off, since in their heart, bullies are quite scared themselves. However, if the bad behaviour continues, you need to get your parents and teachers involved. Don't be afraid to tell them everything without any shame or discomfort. You know how much they care for you. They will know how to deal with the situation. Sharing your experience with someone can also be calming.

Have you unknowingly ever bullied someone? Well, if you have, please know bullying ends up making kids so embarrassed, lonely, sad and afraid that they may even stop behaving like normal kids. Now, you wouldn't wish that for anyone, would you?

Of Crushes and Infatuations

You may find that you have started to think about a particular person too much or feel shy, giggly and self-conscious when they are around. The very mention of their name brings a huge smile to your face. This is called a crush.

You'll have many crushes as you grow older. Don't worry too much about it. It just means you like them a lot, think about them a LOT and want to be around them.

You may have a crush on someone famous, like a musician or an actor. Sometimes you may even have a girl having a crush on an actress. While there is nothing wrong with crushing on a celebrity, it isn't very useful. You don't know them, so you won't be able to meet them and become friends with them. The closest you will ever get is to have them as a wallpaper on your computer. However, having a crush on someone in your class or neighbourhood, can be a whole different thing.

When you chat with your friends, the word boyfriend or girlfriend pops up all the time, doesn't it?

Please note, it is perfectly normal to have many crushes. So, make friends, have fun and talk as much as you like but stay away from anything that could cause you pain and regret later. Particularly, having too much of a physical attraction might become problematic.

How far you want to go is up to you. Is holding hands okay? Is kissing okay? The fact is that your body is undergoing changes which can trigger certain emotions. And though you are no longer a child, you aren't an adult either. Perhaps you will understand relationships better and be able to take a more informed decision in a few years.

Thinking about things in your head is perfectly fine and is probably best. Or write them in your diary. You can read things you felt during your growing up years and smile when you are older.

Expert Advice

Malvika Varma

Peer Pressure

There's a time in everyone's life when friends become your greatest treasures. It seems very important to feel that you belong and fit in with those you like and admire. This is a natural feeling and helps keep a check on ourselves, and get closer to others, which is how great friendships begin. However, if you let this healthy desire to be liked by others turn into a need to be liked, you may find yourself in trouble. You may feel the need for your classmates or friends to accept and appreciate you, to the extent that you may try to be who they want you to be. Peer pressure is when you do things you usually wouldn't and let your choices be directed by others and not yourself. Learning to say no is an essential skill that will help you later, when you are a grown-up. Know that if someone truly cares for you, they won't ask you to do anything you are uncomfortable with. They won't place any conditions on you to prove anything and will appreciate your individuality and choices.

CHAPTER 9

In My Head

Being yourself is all it takes.
If you want to impress someone, don't be someone else, just be yourself.
— Selena Gomez

At your age, the biggest enemy can often be your own mind, driven crazy by hormones. And as you know by now, hormones can cause a lot of confusion. So no matter how overwhelming it may seem now, please remember, this is just a phase. Nevertheless, taking charge of your emotions may be the right thing to do.

Maybe, Maybe Not!

Sometimes we worry too much. Perhaps if we wait, things may sort themselves out.

So, here is a suggestion. Moving along is a better idea than troubling yourself with indecision. You see, indecision is equal to unhappiness. And there is no WRONG or RIGHT. There are just choices. Making one choice may take the other one away, but only for a while. If it's something you truly want, you will find a way to get to it.

For instance, if you want to go to your friend's birthday party, but your parents want you to go to a movie, you could go to your friend's party but ask your parents to watch the movie with you again when it comes on TV. Simple, isn't it?

The Guilt Trip

Guilt is a phenomenon that many girls and women suffer from.

So, what is guilt? It is regret mixed with shame, topped with the feeling of having done something wrong. Sadly, it is often fed into girls from an early age via the supposed ideal of being a 'good girl'.

You are a human being with your own flaws, just like every other person on the planet. Yet, if you don't do your homework on time or aren't good at a subject, you feel or are made to feel less than a 'good girl'. Actually, the idea of a perfect 'good girl' doesn't even exist. Each girl is just a person who is good at some things and not so good at others. The idea is to get to be decent at most things and very good at some others. Trying too hard to be perfect can make you anxious and could stop you from doing better.

So, the next time someone tells you to be a good girl and do something, let them know you are already a great girl! And doing or not doing something will not make you better or worse.

The Rule of 21

The basis of a happy and satisfying life is good habits—mental, physical and emotional.

Science now tells us that making new habits takes twenty-one days of doing something consistently.

Here are some lists you can put up in your room. Looking at them will be a constant reminder and could make it easy for you to follow them.

Good mental habits

1. Not taking too long to decide.
2. Trying and trying until you get better.
3. Becoming a good listener.
4. Staying well-informed about the world around you.
5. Not worrying about things that are out of your control.

Great physical habits

1. Ensuring you get nine to ten hours of deep sleep.
2. Brushing your teeth twice a day, before breakfast and after dinner.
3. Keeping your body and hair very clean.
4. Exercising daily.
5. Spending less time on TV/iPad/phone screens.

Amazing emotional habits

1. Saying sorry if you are wrong.
2. Not making the other person feel bad if they are wrong.
3. Not expecting others to be perfect.
4. Not expecting yourself to be perfect.
5. Having compassion.

It's Okay Not to Be Okay

You may wonder that sometimes when you do nothing, you get great results. At other times, you put in so much hard work and yet fail. Why is this?

The mistake is in the way we look at things. There are no failures because life is a process of learning. Anytime you fail, it only helps you get better. So, the more you fail, the more you learn. Successful people have mastered the art of quickly getting over failure, learning from it and moving on to trying again.

Many actor friends tell me that they give themselves only one weekend to get over a failure. During that time, they feel sorry for themselves, eat junk and blame everyone for their loss. But after that, they snap out of it and try again till they succeed. These are the secrets to success—not being afraid of failure and picking yourself up after you fail.

Blaming others for their failure is a classic loser attitude. And if they can't find anyone to blame, losers blame destiny or God. God and destiny are easy to blame since

no one has seen them. However, the person who blames gets away from doing the hard work.

But you are too smart to blame anyone, I know. You know that if you work hard and smartly, you will get results sooner or later. Knowing you did it yourself is great fun!

Shout Out the Doubt

Shall I speak up, or shall I be quiet? Shall I stand out or blend in? Do I look foolish wearing this or not? Phew!!!

What does one do in that case?

- Talking to someone you trust is a great way to get rid of confusion. Sometimes, answers will come to you even as you describe the situation to a friend.
- Writing a journal or diary is a private way of sorting out your confusion. Answers often appear on the page when you write.

- Talking to your parents may not seem to be the best thing. You may think they won't understand, but remember, they have also gone through puberty, and will get it.
- Talking to the school counsellor is a great idea because they are trained and know exactly what you are going through.
- It is not wise to get advice from the internet. It could vague or way too general and may do more harm than good.

Expert Advice

Emotional Roller Coaster

Hormones play a significant role in mood swings and could cause emotional highs and lows. Psychologists sometimes call this phenomenon the emotional roller-coaster.

Consider our emotions to be a three-legged stool. One factor contributing to what we feel is BIOLOGY. This includes nutrition, sleep and exercise, besides hormones and genetics. The other factor is the ENVIRONMENT, which includes people, events and objects. The third and most important factor is your THINKING!

Yes, the way we perceive things and the meanings we attach to them influences our feelings. What does it say about why we feel the way we do?

Is it the happenings that make us feel what we feel, or is it what we subconsciously think about what happens that makes us feel a certain way?

Think of a situation where a dog shows up on the street. Some people might get terrified if they see a dog around them, some may feel disgusted looking at the dog, and yet others may feel happy. Similarly, you will notice many examples of how people feel differently about the same things. Our emotions are largely self-created; they come from our self-talk, thoughts, perceptions and belief systems. That's good news because that means that we have the power to unlearn them too!

Of course, this doesn't mean that things do not matter at all. It means that we can really add our own masala to situations and events without knowing it, and could end up making things much worse. It's always a better idea to first control what we can, which is our thoughts, rather than try to change external things that are not in our control.

CHAPTER 10

Safe and Sound

The path from dreams to success does exist. May you have the vision to find it.

- Kalpana Chawla

On the internet, anything seems possible. You could post a video of yourself dancing one day, and be offered a soft drink ad the next day. You can see pictures of your childhood home in another city or watch a movie with friends while staying home. There is almost nothing you can't do online.

And that is what makes the web potentially dangerous. It is best to be very careful.

Behind the Screen

For some of us who are introverts, making friends online seems like an easy solution. But is it? Unless the person on the other side of your computer screen is a friend, you will never really know who is chatting with you or even recording your conversations.

It's easy to create a fake online identity. Be very careful because some people are experts at winning a person's trust and leading them to do things they wouldn't otherwise. The golden rule for the internet is to make sure you know people in real life before you start interacting with them online. If anyone asks you to keep your chats 'secret', that should ring an alarm.

Don't ever meet anyone you don't know in real life. Also, don't share personal details such as your home address. You don't want anyone harassing you or your family.

A friend's son got trapped in a drug racket when someone he met online promised him a new cell phone. The poor kid and his family were harassed for months and had to keep going to the cyber crime cell.

You've heard of spam emails, right? These emails often pop up from people or addresses you don't know. Make sure to never click on an email from an unknown address. Even if the offer to click and the curiosity of finding out what's in store is unbearable, remember that clicking on the email can allow hackers to steal important information from your computer.

Sometimes you may also be subject to indecent or violent pictures that can be very unsettling. If this ever happens to you, please tell your parents immediately.

Dangers of Cyberspace

What you put out on your social media accounts is absolutely your choice. It is a reflection of your personality, sense of humour, choices and language.

Do you know that if you put out a photograph, it takes someone just a second to take a screenshot of the picture? This is true for videos too. Recordings can be made without your knowledge.

What seemed like a good idea when you were in a great mood could become an embarrassment later. So, don't send messages or videos that you will regret later.

What you need to remember is that if someone online is pushing you to do something you shouldn't, it's called cyberbullying and it is a punishable crime.

Photo-sharing platforms like Instagram and Facebook are a great way to share your life with friends, but you aren't allowed to do that till you are thirteen years old. And it's best to follow the rules.

Virtual, Not Real

Talking to someone in real life and texting are two *very* different things. When you are with someone, they can see your expressions, body language, what someone else said before you, etc. When the same thing is written down, it can look so different.

What you text and to who you text is important. A casual text can be used out of context by someone who wants to create a problem between you and your friends. A simple photograph can be Photoshopped easily to look like something you never intended.

The sensible thing to do is to keep it real. Our phones and computers are a part of our life, but they cannot replace having a meal, getting a hug or spending quality time with family and friends. Do not mistake the web to be that place.

Staying Safe Online

- Avoid social media till you are thirteen.
- Do not send texts or any other messages to strangers.
- Do not agree to meet strangers.
- Do not accept gifts or freebies.
- Don't get into chat rooms.
- Please don't share your parents' credit card details or use them for purchases online.

- Do not visit websites and add or download apps without your parents' permission.
- Be transparent and share all your online activities with your parents. Do not be secretive.
- Share passwords and email ids with your parents and no one else.
- Don't be friends with strangers while playing online games.
- Do not use real photos online.
- Never post your location on any social media handle. Protect your privacy.

Real Dangers

As we all know, the internet isn't the only unsafe place. The real world can be dangerous as well. You know the rules ... they have been repeated to you a dozen times, but you need to be very careful.

Pranksters often use the ploy of saying that your father or mother has had an accident, to take you elsewhere. These are common ways to lure you out of your comfort area to make you do something you don't want to do. It may sound dramatic, but it could even be to kidnap you. These situations don't just happen in movies or to someone else. They are very real. Any harm to you will hurt not just you but also your entire family—your parents, siblings, grandparents, and even your extended family. So, please be wary of strangers.

Please do not go in dark spaces alone, even if you are playing hide and seek.

Always ensure that you are accompanied by an adult when you visit a public restroom or other public space.

Off-limits!

There are some people who you MUST watch out for. These could be friends of your parents, an uncle, a teacher or even an older cousin. They may try to show extra affection and make you feel special. It could be in the form of compliments, the way they look at you or even the way their hand accidentally brushes you.

Let this alarm you very seriously. Anything that bothers you even slightly must be discussed with your parents.

Let no one make you think it's okay to touch you, make you change in front of them or take you to a lonely spot. The responsibility for the actions they take or are trying to make you take will always be theirs. They are adults and know better. The blame will never be on you.

Make sure to tell this person firmly that you know what they are trying to do, that you won't be a part of it and will report it to your parents or school. Do this at the very beginning, before they involve you in something that makes you uncomfortable.

There are extremely strict laws about an adult trying to touch or take advantage of anyone under the age of eighteen, including imprisonment.

Did You Know?

According to an ancient tradition called Chaupadi, practised by some rural communities in Nepal, women were forced to stay in mud huts or sheds during their periods. It was believed they brought bad luck to their family in those days. Thankfully, this tradition was declared illegal in 2005.

Expert Advice

Feeling Safe and Strong

Feeling safe has many meanings and is a need for us all. Safety isn't just to do with our physical surroundings. We also need to feel emotionally and mentally safe. There are many places, people and situations that make you feel safe, and it is important to recognise them. Some common safe spaces could be your home, your room, your school, the school library, with your parents, grandparents, siblings and friends. See if you can list them down.

You also need to be good at recognising unsafe places, people and situations so that you can be cautious. They may include being isolated or alone, staying out after dark, being alone with an adult you don't know well, at a party where people may be doing things that you are uncomfortable with, in a car when someone is driving rash, being forced into doing something and many more. We must be mindful of these situations and things that make us feel unsafe. Build on your strengths, not just physical but emotional and mental, and rely on them to keep you safe.

Here are some things that can help you stay safe:

1. Always let your parents know where you are going and with whom.
2. Go out in a group if you are going out after dark.
3. Keep emergency phone numbers handy, always.
4. Know about safe and unsafe touch. If anyone (yes, anyone) touches you inappropriately and a voice inside you tells you that it's not okay, you must raise the alarm, shout, scream and call for help loudly. You must immediately inform a person you feel safe with, and your parents.
5. If you find someone following you or staring at you to the extent that it is making you uncomfortable, report it to an adult.

CHAPTER 11

Boys Will Be Boys

As you reach puberty, you may start feeling a little weird around boys. This is perfectly okay. Boys also feel the same around girls when they hit puberty.

Boys are and can be many things other than boyfriends. Dads were boys too, right? So are brothers and cousins.

You may have had some friends who are boys and have been a part of your gang since you were little. Some of them stay friends, but others, who you may have grown up with, start to act all weird.

Sometime now, you or some of your friends may also start to feel shy, tingly and awkward around guys. They were just your pals (annoying ones, maybe) till recently, then what changed?

What changed in you is your hormone called estrogen! It is the same for boys. The production of their hormones called testosterone *(teh-staw-stuh-roun)* indicates that they are also growing up.

Look Who's Changing!

Boys don't get periods but have their share of puberty problems, same as you, but just slightly different. It's easy to see that boys are having a bit of a confusing time, too; they aren't being weird for no reason. Let's see what happens to boys.

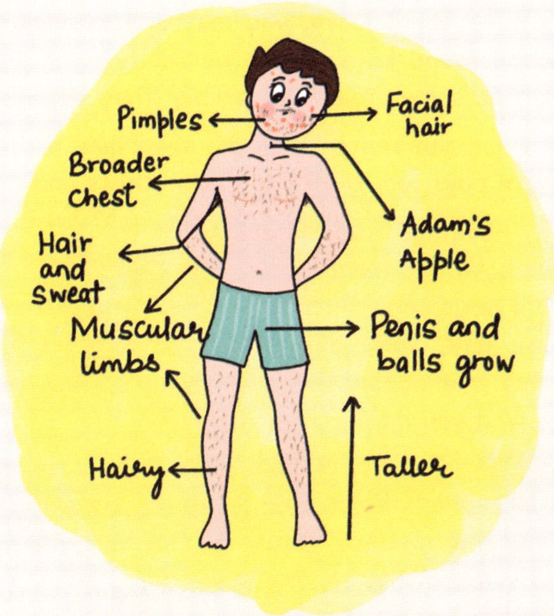

For boys, puberty occurs later than it does for most girls. And when it does, they suddenly shoot up and become much taller than girls in most cases. Their chests and shoulders become broader as their muscles start developing.

Their penis, which is where they pee from, starts to grow bigger. Their testicles or balls (two small sacks on either side below the penis) that store sperm also get bigger.

Hair starts sprouting all over the body, for boys, as it does for you. Besides the appearance of hair in their underarms and the pubic region, moustache hair appears on their upper lip, and there's new fuzzy growth on their chin. The rest of their body also gets hairier than yours.

Another sign of puberty in boys is 'voice breaking'. It is when their voice cracks and goes through a funny grating sort of phase. Often, you will also see an 'Adam's Apple' sticking out from their throat. This bony lump bobs up and down as they speak. Boys get pimples too! Additionally, their sweat glands go into overdrive, causing them to sweat profusely.

Suddenly, the same boys, you may have known since you both were in diapers, become big show-offs. You wonder, what on earth is going on! Well, some of it has to do with you, because you are now noticing boys. And some of it has to do with them; they are growing up to become adults too.

The male hormones often make boys rowdier and louder and evoke more feelings towards girls or other boys. But this is natural because they, too, are going through a new phase in their lives.

Boys also try to attract your attention by doing crazy things like wheelies on their bikes or arm-wrestling to show they are 'stronger' than the rest. You can smile and join in the fun, for they mean no harm.

Expert Advice

Puberty and Boys

You read about how the hypothalamus triggers the pituitary gland, which then releases two hormones—FSH AND LH—that help develop the reproductive organs in both girls and boys during puberty. The hormones travel to ovaries in girls, and in boys, they stimulate the testes in the scrotum to start producing the male hormone testosterone, which results in changes in a boy's body at the time of puberty. Testosterone also helps to make sperm that will fertilise an egg to make babies.

CHAPTER 12

You're a Hero!

The idea of what a young lady can be has changed drastically over the years. That is good news because now the world is open to all your crazy, mad, fun and bright new ideas.

Some things are, however, important at all times.

Girls Aren't Boys

Some girls think being free is being like a man because they have only seen men and boys being free. This is just silly. Girls are girls, and boys are boys, each different, and each with their unique qualities. It is often said, men are physically stronger and women are emotionally. It's like an apple trying to compete with an orange. There is simply no competition.

I believe, being a girl means to be strong in spirit and mind, determined to make a life you can be proud of.

Some girls cry or act all helpless to get their work done. That isn't very smart. Why should you cry to get something done?

In older times, girls needed men to protect them, but that isn't the case now. The stories that you've heard of princesses needing princes to rescue them were of a time when girls didn't go to school or had jobs and supported their families. You, of course, are part of a new breed of girls, who not only take care of themselves but also of the men and women around them.

I see you as a strong warrior, who can protect herself and others, too, with your intelligence, humour and quick thinking. Your ability to listen and feel others' pain is nature's gift to you.

No Means No

Many girls find it hard to say 'no' even when they really don't want to do something. They then end up doing what they didn't want to and feel worse. It is best to learn to say 'no', politely, but firmly. It isn't wise to get swept away by the flow and then regret it.

In my opinion, the best option is to ask for time. Think about what you want to do and then decide.

Mostly, saying 'no' by giving your reasons for not doing something works best with close friends and family. With others, you may simply say you don't want to do it because you are uncomfortable.

Saying no does not mean it's the end of a friendship; it is the sign of a friendship that can be comfortable for both friends.

Stand Up for Yourself

It wasn't okay for girls to study or wear what they wanted or even step out without covering their heads, until recently. Girls and women before us have fought hard for years, just so we may have these fundamental rights today.

Malala Yousafzai, a Pakistani girl, was shot at while trying to go to school. Luckily, Malala survived and is still fighting hard to get Pakistani girls the right to study.

Another teenager, Greta Thunberg from Sweden, shook the world up by demanding that politicians address climate change more seriously. Inspired by her voice, millions of students worldwide protested in their own countries for environmental reforms.

Many other girls and women are fighting hard for making the world fairer for all of us.

Please become strong with a deep respect for the huge reserve of strength nature has given you as a girl. Do not let other girls down. Stand up and speak up for what you believe to be correct. Discover your own power and make the world better for everyone around you.

Snowflake Girl

Did you know that each snowflake that has ever fallen out of the sky in any part of the world since the beginning of time has a different design? It's so hard to imagine millions and billions of different designs!

Now, look at the people you meet—each one has a unique voice, face, body and a different nature.

Nature meant for us to be different—one of a kind.

While it is fun to follow fashion trends, it is so cool to develop your own way of doing things. You don't want to look like a copy of someone else, do you?

Your body, voice, face and nature will find its own comfort and style, be it clothes, hair or the way you talk.

This is your age to explore and experiment with yourself. Try new things, listen to new music and explore new places with your family.

You are at an important crossroads in life. You are cementing your identity. It is much more than how you look or what you score in school. It is more about how you think, care for friends and family, the ambitions you have, etc.

For many years I collected coloured stones. I washed and cleaned them with care, and there was a pile of sparkly clean, beautiful rocks from every place I visited. Each stone had a name and a story. My parents thought I was crazy, but they never stopped me. Soon, I had seven or eight friends who began collecting stones, and we would get together and exchange stones. Their stories also changed as they changed owners.

We eventually had a small community of stone collectors and we even had some teachers who joined us on our stone and rock-collecting trips. It became a thing!

Another friend used to make clothes for pets, as a little girl. Today, she has her own business and is doing exceedingly well. Guess what her business is? Yup, she makes personalised clothes and accessories for pets.

Do whatever you were put on earth to do—your heart will guide you to whatever that unique thing is. Remembering that it has to be of use to others and yourself is the best way.

I hope it will lead you to a life full of joy.

With all my love.

Always,

T

(You can call me that. We are friends now, aren't we?!)

Expert Advice

Speak Up!

We all have been given a voice and a mind of our own. But only a few people think they can use their voice to state their opinions, thoughts and feelings. Many people are over-concerned about whether they are saying the right thing, being laughed at or disagreed with, being perceived as impolite or offending someone, or they don't think that their thoughts are important enough to be expressed. Often, being passive is passed on as being polite, and being aggressive gets you nowhere. But being assertive is the art and skill of communicating in a way that you grant yourself the right to speak up for yourself when something unfair is happening or when something isn't in your interest. But you need to do it in a way that is firm and respectful to others too. You need to speak to others about yourself in a way you would want to be spoken to.

Acknowledgements

To say I am grateful to my parents is a huge understatement. They gave me an upbringing that was so focused on curiosity that a new challenge is the mainstay of my life. So thank you, mum and dad.

Deepest gratitude to my in-laws, who are always up for any of my new adventures.

A big thank you to Sanjay, my husband and best friend, who is my constant sparring partner in all things creative.

To Vidhi Bhargava, without whom there would be no book. She had the idea, pushed me to write and held my hand through all my shenanigans. And Akanksha Agnihotri, for enriching the book with her joyful doodles.

Dr Mala knows me since I was a teenager and has been our family's guiding spirit forever. Malvika Varma is a treasure of my life—friend, philosopher and the keeper of my life's compass. Thank you both, for enriching this book with the depth of your experience and sound guidance.

To all the mommies in the various mommy groups, thank you for always having my back and the sisterhood of moms that enables me to bring up my Tara with so many wise suggestions.

And finally, a big thank you to the most precious gift of all—my daughter Tara. She is a genuine creative nut, with the funkiest imagination that keeps me on my toes!

About the Author

Actor, author and filmmaker Tisca Chopra is fondly known for her memorable performance as the loveable mother from *Taare Zameen Par*. A passionate storyteller and performer, Tisca's every endeavour has been loved and awarded. She has acted in over fifty feature films in different languages with eminent directors like Aamir Khan, Sudhir Mishra and Shoojit Sircar.

As someone who's always refused to settle for the mediocre, Tisca's insistence on excellence and passion have not only won her acclaim and fame but also two Filmfare Awards, as well as recognition globally in both, films and on stage, at the New York International Film Festival and the Toronto Film Festival. She recently turned filmmaker—writing and producing award-winning and critically acclaimed short films like *Chutney*, and her directorial debut—*Rubaru*.

Tisca has created a singular path to showcase the idea of rising above barriers and sparking conversation around socially sensitive topics through filmmaking and writing. Her short films have been about breaking traditional perceptions of female characters and roles and creating a distinct, authentic narrative. She carries this unique voice to her writing and off-screen persona as well.

She is set to direct her feature film later this year.

Beyond her acting career, Tisca has worked with Sam Pitroda on the National Knowledge Commission to revamp the education system. She works consistently with NGOs and small businesses to give a leg up to women entrepreneurs.

She lives in Mumbai with her pilot-writer husband Sanjay, and eight-year-old daughter Tara.

About the Illustrator

Akanksha Agnihotri is an illustrator based in Delhi. She loves all things colourful, cartoony and crafty. She loves to read, take naps and daydream besides travelling and exploring nature. Her favourite pastime is making quirky doodles about everyday life and sharing them on her popular Instagram handle @doodlesndreams.

About the Contributors

Dr Mala Arora is one of the topmost obstetricians and gynaecologists in Delhi. With more than thirty years of experience, she is an expert in infertility & IVF, recurrent abortions, menopause & endoscopic surgery. She has been a fellow at the Royal College of Obstetricians and Gynaecologists (UK) and holds a Diploma in Obstetrics and Diploma in Anesthesia from Ireland and United Kingdom, respectively. She has authored the book *Recurrent Pregnancy Loss* and has received five gold medals including the best award for the year 1978. She has been the president of Federation of Obstetric and Gynaecological Societies of India.

Malvika Varma has been practising as a counselling psychologist since 2009. She has a Master's degree in psychology from Mumbai and is trained in Cognitive Behavioral Therapy (CBT) and Rational Emotive Behaviour Therapy (REBT). Born in Lucknow, she grew up in Noida, set up her practice in Mumbai and is now living in idyllic Vancouver with her husband (read best friend). When she isn't working, you will most likely find her in the kitchen obsessing over her latest culinary interests. She loves to bike, hike, read, watch movies and spend time with family and friends.